The Song

of the

Shulamite

(Secrets of an Irresistible Woman)

By
Sharon Ramkhelawan

PublishAmerica
Baltimore

First printing

ISBN: 1-4137-5942-4

PUBLISHED BY PUBLISHAMERICA, LLLP

www.publishamerica.com

Baltimore

Printed in the United States of America

*This book is dedicated to my mother
Who is effortlessly irresistible...every day,
and who always believed in me.*

Acknowledgments

Special thanks to my husband Curtis,
I try harder because you inspire me,
I love you.

My dad, thanks for believing in my calling.

Jude,
the most talented, caring
and supportive person I know.

Jason, who said,
"I know you have ideas,
don't use those,
use the revelations
the Lord has given you." I did, J!

Danielle, Petal and Rose:
You inspire me and probably don't know it!

Bishop Kevin and Mrs. Diana Taylor
and my family at Victory Temple.

Contents

Secrets of an irresistible woman

The chandelier-lit room is full of people socializing, communicating and looking busy when she enters the doorway. At first, only the person at the door notices her walk in, and he is transfixed …her beautiful face, her incredible gown, her gorgeous hair, her flawless skin…she is irresistible. Then, like a wave it spreads across the room as each person turns to gaze toward her in an endeavor to see what caught their companies' attention. With every eye on her, she stands there oblivious to the fact that everyone thinks she is the most beautiful woman they have ever laid eyes on. The men are enchanted, some women are envious, and all are impressed.

I dare say this daydream has crossed your mind in one form or another at some time in your life with you, of course, being the irresistible woman. The desire to be admired, complimented and sometimes even envied has been the driving force of many a woman's make up regimen and wardrobe. It's also the reason why many women strive to emulate the icons on television and in magazines often setting unreasonable and unlikely standards for their physical appearance. The media has propagated stereotypes of what the perfect woman should look like, but an irresistible woman is an entirely different concept. I'm not going to tell you that it's only what's on the inside that makes you irresistible, because more often that not, human beings will not get beyond your physical appearance in the first meeting. And if there is no interest in the first meeting, then there is little hope for a second or third. Irresistibility exists on more than one level, and it comes in the package of a complete person. The Bible, which has answers to any question that we may ask, has given us the true secrets of the irresistible woman and they're found in the Songs of Solomon.

These secrets are not about being the best that you can be…you've heard all that before. Sometimes the best we can be will fall far below our own and other's expectations of us. This is about being the best. Period. Among all women, being the one that the most eligible bachelor wants. Being the one that your husband constantly dreams of and is moved to poetry at the thought of. Being the one that is undeniably irresistible. The Bible gives us an example of such a woman. This is what the Shulamite was. She was indelibly imprinted on King Solomon's mind and in his heart. When he could have any woman he wanted (and he did), she was the one he desired most. Our minds may picture the Shulamite as an exquisitely shaped, size-four bombshell with long legs and full lips etc., perhaps closely resembling some exotic movie star or model…Perhaps we think that she was demure and soft-spoken, almost angelic in appearance so no man could resist. That perhaps is beauty, but irresistibility insists on much more.

There were certain characteristics about the Shulamite that made her irresistible. To the surprise of many, we are informed in the Songs of Solomon that she wasn't the most physically attractive, she wasn't the most talented or the wealthiest but the King could not get her off his mind. The qualities that the Shulamite did possess, however, are the same ones that make some women irresistible today, the same ones that if you apply them to yourself and your lifestyle, you will begin a noticeable and amazing transformation in youself. It is this level of beauty, true irresistibility, that God used to describe the bride that He himself is looking for. It's irresistibility that makes you attractive to your spouse, to your peers, to everyone around you and to your God.

Is your love is better than wine?

L ove is like a tender rose some people say. Over decades and centuries, love has been compared to many varied things. From "love is a battlefield" to "love is a many splendid thing" there has been no more popular topic for poetry, prose, song or fable. It has been compared to everything under the sun, indeed even the sun. In the Songs of Solomon, love is compared to wine. The king and the Shulamite often refer to love being better than wine. Rightly understood, wine in the Songs of Solomon was a symbol of lavishness, wealth, joy and celebration. And to Solomon the love of the Shulamite was far more than this.

Wine is intoxicating. If not abused it calms your nerves, soothes your woes (Ps 104:15), makes you bold, quenches your thirst, makes you giddy, alleviates your pain (Luke 10:34), enhances the taste of your food and is pleasant to smell and taste. All of these things are implied in the qualities of wine. No other substance can do all of this without creating illusions, expectations and irreparable damage to your mind. The love of the Shulamite, however, far surpassed the qualities of wine for the king, and this was just another of the things that made her an irresistible woman.

If the irresistible woman's love causes a man to overlook wine, then the opposite, the unappealing woman, would drive a man to the bottle. Sound familiar? How many husbands run to the bottle to drown their woes and forget their sorrows? The Bible demonstrates here that having a love that soothes, calms, reassures, alleviates pain, and is appealing, refreshing and even addictive is a part of being irresistible. By no means am I suggesting that behind every barroom drunkard is a woman who is not irresistible or incapable of loving. There are certainly many people who have alcohol strongholds in their lives that have nothing to do with their spouses. I believe, however, that there are many men who are driven to find the comforts that a wife is intended to provide in all the wrong places.

Classical conditioning, history and society have made many women overly dependent on sympathy and created in some of us a victim mentality despite our obvious strength. In fact, we equate the two in that the more of a victim you are, the stronger you seem to be. We see women who have been abused or otherwise traumatized as being stronger than women who have not had to deal with some of these issues. But no one can honestly accuse a mother in a nuclear family of being weaker than a single mom just because she did not face the same struggles. Maybe in a similar situation, that "nuclear mom" would also rise to the occasion and do whatever was necessary to provide for her children or even save her life. Just because her circumstances were different, it does not necessarily mean that she is weaker. Your real strength does not lie in the severity of your circumstance. In this world it is in your ability to rise up above the circumstance. That's the measure of your true natural strength. In Christ, however, real strength goes beyond your ability to rise above, because sometimes there is no way humanly possible to get out of a situation. It is at the point of our weakness and of hopelessness that we become truly strong, for we can tap in to the greatest strength that exists. God said that his strength is made perfect in our weakness, and Paul said, "I will boast in my weakness that Christ's power will rest upon me…for when I am weak then am I strong." That happens only when we realize that we can't handle it on our own, and we cry out for the hand of God – when it finally dawns on us that working our hands to the bone to support our family, laboring thanklessly for a small salary or never having a second of time for yourself is absolutely enough reason to reach for the strong hand of your Father. Remember, it's not by your might or power but by the Spirit of God that you can face that situation and overcome it. God takes your overworked, exhausted body and "the Lord, your God, will make you most prosperous in all the work of your hands." He takes your overwhelmed mind and guards it with the peace of God, which surpasses all understanding. He heals your heart, which has been broken or which has been turned into stone, and recreates it into the heart that is capable of love that is better than wine.

A woman who is irresistible is a strong woman. Human strength is limited and finite; it is attainable and resistible. Only in the perfection of God's strength does this bloom into irresistibility. A woman living in the strength and power of Almighty God is a woman of undefeatable spirit and strength. There need not be a lot of noise and clamor around it. The strength of the world depends on noise to appear powerful. Just watch professional wrestlers on TV and you'll understand what I mean. The louder the bark or growl, the stronger they appear. A strong woman is not necessarily the one who gets in the face of the public or her family and screams, hollers and protests. Noise is not a gauge of strength. God's strength is deep and profound, working in the innermost parts of our souls, changing, equipping and illuminating. It may not be loud, but it is most noticeable to everyone among you. What people will admire in you as great strength will actually be the strength of the spirit of God in you. It is what sets you apart from every other strong woman. A strength that is inexhaustible, amazing and perfect. The Psalmist David was awed by the strength of Almighty God. Understandably so, since even as a boy, David was used by God to defeat the giant Goliath. But even as a boy, David believed in the strength that had nothing to do with his own muscle or willpower and everything to do with the power of the Creator of the universe. "You come to me with swords and spears, but I come in the name of the Lord of Hosts," was David's bold-faced cry towards the mighty monster. David at that moment was the object of all of Israel's attention. But not because of his boldness…for they must have thought that was his stupidity. But the second that monstrosity hit the dirt, David became irresistible to the people of Israel. They celebrated him more than their beloved king and sang praises in his honor. That was the point at which David became *impossible to resist or withstand the force or effect of, or impossible to refuse, oppose or avoid because he was too pleasant, attractive and strong.* The kid that killed the giant! That's someone you'd want to be friends with! You'd certainly want him on your team. What a salesman he would make! Just think about the hordes of females that would grow weak at the sight of him. He could probably have had his pick…he was irresistible because he was wise enough to rely on the abundant strength of God. No one could deny it, especially not his older brother who had previously accused him of being a little snooper trying to check out the "big people's battle." I smile when I think about the face of that same bother as David turned around and looked at him when the huge enemy came crashing down. He would forever think twice about putting David down.

This irresistibility stretches far beyond the reaches of the object of your affection and those you want most to please. Even though you may only want your husband or fiancé or friend to find you irresistible, other people can't help but notice when you are. The Shulamite was irresistible to Solomon, but she captivated even the other people in the court. In Sol 1:4, the daughters of Jerusalem, the other women in Solomon's court, the women of incredible beauty who had been primped and pampered said to the Shulamite, "We will be glad and rejoice in you. We will remember your love more than wine!" Remember these women were not her childhood friends…she was their competition! But when God makes you irresistible, not even your enemies can dislike you. Even your enemies will find you irresistible. Is that incredible or what? Even the other women declared that they would remember the Shulamite's love more than wine. Many people say maybe they were just echoing Solomon's sentiments, but how often do you hear women who are vying for one man's attention sing the praises of one of their competitors? Like David, those that doubt, despise or are competing against you cannot deny the truth. They realized that the love of the Shulamite was better than wine itself to get Solomon in the mood to court, to adore and become passionate about someone. She was someone they could not forget. Can people say that about you? Is your love better than wine?

Ask yourself these questions on this "love that is better than wine scale" and see where you rate. Be honest and think about particular situations and different people who you love. On a scale of 1to 10

How refreshing is my love?

You're 10 if-People who you love feel revived and encouraged in your company or by your advice. They leave smiling and happy that you're in their lives. Your love is filled with optimism and reassurance even when it seems unwarranted. You do not rejoice in your loved one's pain and being the bearer of bad news, even if it proves that you were right all along.

1-People who you love become agitated, tired or discouraged in your company or by your advice. They leave saddened…even if it's because they can't see you until tomorrow. You get a bit of sordid pleasure when they're unhappy because you are not there. The unhappier they are, the better you feel, the more loved you feel.

How calming and soothing is my love?

10-You make the ones you love feel calm, relaxed and tranquil after their day, even if yours was harder. You ask and suggest in love. You allow time to relax or a moment to recuperate. You encourage and support. Spending time with you makes those you love feel like they're on a mini-vacation.

1-You make those you love feel forced, flustered and obligated to work as you do, constantly keeping them on the edge about money, jobs, relationships and treating you right. You're commanding and aggressive...often leading to fighting and quarrels. You have him walking on eggshells trying not to upset you. Then, you get mad that he's being so cautious.

How healing is my love?

10-The ones you love feel better in painful times because of you. From a bruised knee to a bruised ego, you make it appear less critical but still give it your undivided attention. Even if it was your husband's fault that the check bounced, you don't make him feel worse when he already feels terrible.

1-The ones you love feel sorry for themselves or sorry for the way they think they're affecting you. Instead of hubby feeling better, he feels worse because he's hurt you so badly and now you can't get that haircut, especially since you're so "understanding" that he messed up the check book. He condemns himself and that makes you feel much better. You use tears to get to your family and guilt them into misery over how much they hurt you.

How appetizing is my love?

10- Your love encourages those around you to long to be around you. You are sweet and satisfying in word, thought and deed. People want you to talk more, and it's not just you liking the sound of your own voice. You don't prattle idly but are heard when you have a sensible contribution to make, so your opinion is always valued. Your voice is sweet to your husband or family or friend, and sometimes when you're quiet he wishes you could say something.

1- You are criticizing, cautious and even callous. You sometimes can ruin an entire meal in one fell swoop. You know they're thinking, "I wish she would be quiet." You are smothering and demanding, jealous and insecure. You are apt to "fly off the handle" over minor issues and sometimes even try to implement "rules" he needs to abide by to make the relationship work "better."

How intoxicating is my love?

10- Your affection for those you love makes a hard day seem worth it to them. Your spouse or friend says that it was difficult to not think about you. You "make the world go away," and coming home to you is the highlight of their day.

1-Those around you are glad for some "space" because they keep getting in your way, annoying you or disturbing you. Coming home or going out with you is a bit of a risk. They might do something you don't like.

Well…how did you do? I believe most of us would have generously given ourselves a couple tens or maybe mostly nines or eights. While it is not possible to be tens ALL of the time and in every circumstance, irresistibility resides in the tens. When these characteristics are no longer an effort for you, but makeup the person you are…you're on your way.

"There's no way I can do that!" I hear you screaming at me in your mind. "You just don't know my husband! My kids are crazy!" I hear you loud and clear and I believe you. There really is NO way you can do it, but it CAN be done. That's where surrender comes in. That's where, "It's not by might, nor by power but by my spirit says the Lord of hosts," comes in. You can't do it, but He can do it. He can do it through you. Our God specializes in taking the rough and unrefined and creating precious gems and priceless treasure.

I have been fortunate to grow up and work among many women who have allowed the Holy Spirit to do this refiner's work in their lives. My godmother Samdai, my mother Kisundai, my pastor's wife Diana, and many others are irresistible women. Heads turn when my mother or my pastor's wife walk into a room. The same happened with my godmother when she was still alive. They are not only beautiful on the outside, but there is an indescribable grace, unparalleled elegance and undeniable delicacy that emanates from all of them. Furthermore, the power and knowledge of God overshadows them and when they speak…people listen. I have never heard my mother bicker with other women or speak evil about another, not even to my father. She laughs and everyone else laughs right along because you can tell she's laughing from way down in her belly. If she cries, it breaks the heart of everyone around because her strength is an eminent aspect of her personality. She assists the young and old in every way she can and offers the identical courtesy of a truly attentive ear to whomever needs it. Her advice is sound and always rooted in the truth of God's word; her intelligence and maturity are trusted and respected. In the above "Better than wine" scale…. she is in every way a 10. She will be the first to tell you that anything she is that's good is a product of God's merciful kindness.

Having love that is better than wine is one of the characteristics of irresistibility. You replace the need for artificial balms and mood enhancers. The Shulamite brought joy to her love but also to all those around her. Does this describe you? Sometimes it's easy to please and love those we love, but what about those that we don't necessarily care for? How do they feel in your presence? Indifferent? Awful? The Shulamite gained admirers among her competition, and she did it without effort. She didn't set out to make everyone like her. Irresistibility is not a talent; it's a personality trait. If you also make the people you don't necessarily care for feel comfortable, what then, about the ones who have done you wrong? Do you go out of your way to make them miserable? Do you hold a grudge or harbor bitterness toward them? This is one of the most effective tools to keep you ineffective with less impact than you were meant to have in this world. Bitterness is like cancers that destroy you and do nothing to the person you are bitter toward.

The Shulamite had every reason to be bitter toward her mother's sons. She said, "My mother's sons were angry with me and made me take care of their vineyards, so my own vineyard I have not kept." Her brothers occupied her with their duties and chores so much that she was unable to take care of herself. Yet even to them she was not bitter, and in turn they loved and protected her. "What shall we do for our sister in the day she is spoken for? If she is a wall, we will build upon her a battlement of silver, and if she is a door, we will enclose her with boards of cedar." Her brothers are very protective of her because they are very aware of her value. This is not only a powerful commentary about the Shulamite's sexual purity until the day of her marriage but of the hedge of protection God builds around those who fear Him. Are you in a position where those you love find you irresistible, those who are supposed to be your enemies can't help but be your supporters, and those who you should dislike are not a burden of bitterness to you? If you're not, then you're at the perfect spot in your life to fix that. Right now you are like clay in the hand of an Almighty God. Clay that is too hard and resistant or packed with broken glass and pieces of stone cannot be molded into a proper vessel. Clay that is malleable, changeable and willing becomes magic in the hands of the potter. Let's pray this repair prayer together…A prayer for God to teach you to love truly and deeply, perfectly and unconditionally…the way He loves.

Dear Father,

Thank you for your perfect love, which you have given to me. Thank you for first loving me, even while I was yet a sinner. Today I give you my heart, which has been mishandled and mistreated. Take it and mend it. Repair the pieces that may be chipped and erase all the stains of past hurt that it might harbor. Create in me a clean heart Oh God, renew a right Spirit within me. Place in me your perfect love that alleviates all fear.

In Jesus name,
Amen

If you prayed that prayer sincerely, the Holy Spirit will empower you with the ability to put this love into practice. Start today, and do not be discouraged if it doesn't seem to be changing immediately. Just watch yourself become more irresistible every day as you practice a love that is better than wine.

Tasting this true love for the first time is a giddy experience, and many people are caught off guard. Your family will look at you differently and so will your co-workers or classmates and friends. They may suspect you of ulterior motives or even think you've finally fallen off your rocker. Just a little at a time is usually all it takes to see the full picture though. Just a simple kindness to your tired husband this afternoon, or a date with your spouse in which you do NOT become irritated will be like a breath of fresh air; it's almost like wine tasting. If you had to truly taste wine, you'd pour a little in a glass and then swish it around in a circular motion so that the fragrance is slowly forced upward in the centrifugal motion. You let the fragrance waft past your nostrils and breathe it in naturally. You would not snuffle it up in one quick sniff, but let the fragrance itself travel. Then, when your taste buds are tingling and your head is filled with its pleasant aroma, you lift the glass to your taste buds and slowly let a small measure of the fragrant liquid slide past your teeth and on your tongue. As your mouth closes, relish how the taste is entwined with the aroma that previously filled your head. Feel how the scent and the taste combine to form the round fullness of the wine and realize that both are necessary for the wine to be completely satisfying.

Experiencing love in its purest form for the first time is like the experience of trying this new wine. (SOS 2:13) Even before it reaches maturity, it is good, and even before its full effect takes place on your loved ones, they will notice the change. A little to start with is all it takes, but just a taste always leaves you wanting more. So don't be afraid to practice. Maybe your family might think you've gone crazy, but that might not be such a bad thing.

My one is THE ONLY ONE (SOS 6:8-9)

King Solomon was by far the most desirable man in his day. Not only was he gorgeous to look at, as evidenced by the Shulamite's passionate descriptions of his physique, "arms like beams of gold and his body like polished ivory…legs like pillars of marble," and the wisest man who walked the planet, a stunning orator and judge, but he was rich. Not just millionaire status "live comfortably rich" but excessively and abundantly prosperous. Solomon was almost every woman's dream man. It is curious that the work for which Solomon is most remembered, however, is a love song written in praise of one woman: the Shulamite. One woman captured his heart and attention to the point that he was moved to poetry and his feelings for her were so intense that those words are a reflection of the way the God himself feels toward his bride. Have you ever left an imprint on someone's heart that was so deep it could stand the test of centuries of time?

Why would Solomon favor this Shulamite above his choice of hundreds of women? Why did Solomon write this particular passionate and sensual Song? What was it about the Shulamite and Solomon's affection for her that made this passion comparable to that between Christ and the church, God and you? Solomon remarked: *"There are sixty queens, eighty concubines, and virgins without number. My dove, my perfect one, **is the only one,** the only one of her mother, the favorite of the one who bore her."*(SOS 6: 8-9)

Something about the Shulamite captured Solomon's attention, made him long for her when he had the love of every woman he wanted, and made him see her as a "perfect one, the only one." She was irresistible to him.

The Shulamite didn't have access to love potion #9 nor was she privy to the nipping, tucking, botoxing, peeling, de-stressing, finishing, cosmetizing, coloring, and accenting that many women can avail themselves of in a quest for irresistibility. All of these things in many instances can lead to more

19

beautification, but none of them are responsible for irresistibility. Before we go on any farther, ask yourself this question, "Why do I want to be irresistible?" Is it to acquire a certain type of mate? To make sure that your spouse is never unfaithful to you? To be more popular in school, in church, at work? To have people fawn over you and compliment you everywhere you go? To make your husband pay for taking you for granted? Maybe you think that you will get more "stuff" more easily? There are countless reasons why a person would want to be irresistible, but these are the same ones that would drive you farther and farther away from your goal.

Have you ever heard someone say, "She's hot and she knows it?' That is often said about extremely beautiful women, but seldom, if ever, about irresistible ones. All of the above rationales for wanting to be irresistible suggest that you are very aware of yourself and your effect on people. This type of individual is usually easy to resist. If they come off as snobbish, or pretentious or even conceited...irresistibility is a lost cause. "Irresistible" according to Miriam Webster means *"impossible to resist or withstand the force or effect of or impossible to refuse, oppose or avoid because too pleasant, attractive or strong."* Too pleasant? Does that describe any of the people you know who think they are irresistible? Probably not. Herein lies one of the secrets: Irresistibility is always in the heart of the beholder. Unlike beauty in the eyes, irresistibility seeps past the eyes and mind and wrestles the heart. It is at this point that you become unforgettable, irrefutable, unavoidable and uncharacteristically attractive to another. This is what the Shulamite was to Solomon. His sleepless nights, lingering daydreams and wistful thoughts were centered on the woman who had not only pleased his eyes but also captured his heart.

A beautiful woman will leave an impression on someone's mind, and probably remain on their mind for hours, days...maybe even years. That is a strong impression until the next beautiful woman comes along. An irresistible woman slips past your mind and makes an impact on your heart. That impression cannot be replaced. It is like a fingerprint because irresistibility cannot be copied. It is a character trait of the possessor that is created only by the unique facets of her life that make her who she is. Copying someone else's smile or mannerisms will not enhance her beauty because everything she is, is perfectly suited to her. She is "the only one." Leaving an impression on someone's heart may begin with a simple smile, but it cannot stop there. To move a person's heart requires an act of selflessness. To give of yourself without expecting a reward is one of the strongest ways to leave an impression on a heart. By this I don't mean volunteering at the homeless shelter and gaining the respect and admiration of your family and peers. It's about giving your time and energy to those who need it and not caring if people know about it. It's selflessness without showiness. This was one of the habits of the Shulamite. She worked for the sake of others, sometimes neglecting her own comfort. (SOS 6) Do you know anyone with that kind of heart? They help others while not gaining recognition or acknowledgment for their labor...without complaining? They're the types who don't need the "volunteer" badge because they consider it their duty and privilege to be of service in obedience to Almighty God. The scarcity of this type of servanthood is one of the reasons why irresistible people are in such meager supply.

Last night I watched a little bit of the Miss USA beauty pageant. In the beginning as the girls strutted out in their similar dresses proudly parading and representing their respective states, one thing was unmistakable: they were trying to make an impression. Every one of them wanted those judges to look past their bodies and see something more. Why? Because every girl in that pageant had an enviably fit and toned body, a beautiful face with dazzling white smiles, and the same flattering outfit. If they all wore the same dress and from neck down were almost identical...and had pretty faces and great teeth, what on earth would make them stand out? Behind the flashy smiles and twinkling eyes was almost an appeal for the judges to look and see more in them than they did in the rest. I think that's the reason why I always tend to favor the contestant who looks a bit different from all the rest. The variety is strangely refreshing. But these contestants have been trained to give the judges what they expect. They know what the past winners did and coaches drill these traits into them. The teary "thank you so much" with outstretched palms that they send the judges' way as they advance to the next round is almost always a practiced tactic that demonstrates their gratitude and appreciation, that they hope will warm the judges heart. Some take the all-American-girl approach; others the innocent country beauty and still others the intelligent modern bombshell, but the point is to make an impression.

Yet, do any of these girls become *impossible to resist or withstand the force or effect of; or impossible to refuse, oppose or avoid because too pleasant, attractive or strong?* If anyone did then there would be no contest would there? Well, this is what the Shulamite in the Song of Solomon was. She probably would not look like the other contestants; in fact, she did not look like the women in Solomon's courts. But she didn't waste a minute trying to look like anyone else. If she did, then she would automatically become "one of them" instead of "the only one." Are you "the only one?" I can almost hear the sarcasm in some replies, "Yeah and thank God I am, cause the world couldn't stand two of me!" or "Yes, I'm the only one, but I wish I was another only one instead." Recognizing that you are unique and not being distressed by that is the first step toward irresistibility. You might think you'd look better with that other person's nose, but that would be the a copy of their nose, not yours. If your desire is to improve the way you look, why not strive to make yourself the best you? You are the only one who God made exactly like you inside and out. All of the things about you make you an individual. I once heard John Hagee say, "God made you an original. Why die a cheap copy of someone else?" While all originals are not irresistible, every irresistible person is certainly without exception…an original.

Colorful women and women of color
(SOS 1:5)

Colorful and set apart. See your difference as a blessing, a salutation of separation! A declaration of difference! Not as a flaw, hindrance or setback. Whatever seems like an obstacle is going to become your stepping stone.

Every one of us can think about something in ourselves that we would like to change. Some things are more temporary and easier to change than others and as women we believe that we would feel better about ourselves if we had them. Sometimes we feel like these "differences" hinder us from achieving certain goals or being as successful as we could have been without them. What do you wish you could change? Your height? Weight? The size of your nose or other body parts? The color of your skin? I grew up hearing my friends say, "I wish I were just a few shades lighter," or "He'll have nothing to do with her ...she's too dark." In our West Indian society, it almost seemed like an unspoken rule: the lighter your skin, the prettier you were. As a young teen, my brown complexion was becoming a hindrance to me and seeds of bitterness and envy would spring up when lighter-skinned girls who I felt were less intelligent got the important parts in the plays, the extra attention from teachers and everything else I felt I deserved. For a while I let that bitterness dictate my attitude. My countenance fell when I would walk into a room and fairer people were there, because I was certain that no one would notice me, and I was usually right since I was sitting aside, alone in my sulky chair. I was everything but irresistible.

Whether we like to admit it or not, many of us still feel handicapped by the color of our skin. It may be that we think we're a bit too dark or a tad too pale or too ashen or too red. We may not be social cripples, but there is certainly a limp there that stems from feeling like we may not be treated with the same attention as another. Much of this may be blamed on classical conditioning and maybe even our childhoods and past experiences, but the fact is that it is largely because of the way we see ourselves. It is a limp that's there just out of habit. It's as if we had a broken ankle three years ago and the limp has not gone away because we are nervous about putting weight on the "bad foot." You may have had a bad experience that related to the color of your skin three years ago and to this day you tread lightly and cautiously. Your defenses are up and you're on guard, never allowing yourself to be fully comfortable, trusting and walking with the confidence that you should. You don't discriminate; you just don't want to be discriminated against.

Though the Shulamite was an irresistible woman, she did not fit into the stereotype of the beautiful woman of her day. She was not the fragile courtier who never worked and spent her days being pampered and perfumed. She did not dwell in the palace of the king, eating their food and sitting in the shade of his royal courts. In Solomon's day the light-skinned women were considered beautiful and more so if they were without flaws of blemish or spot. That could happen if you did nothing all day but lounged around in the shade being bathed in oil and spices...away from biting insects, any manual labor and almost any outdoor activity. The Shulamite did not fit into any of those categories. And it is here that her wisdom seems to match that of her beloved Solomon in that she recognized that this difference was not her handicap but her triumph.

She knew exactly who she was. She did not go to the king's palace to compare herself to any of the daughters of Jerusalem. She certainly made no attempt to be like them. Neither did she in any way attempt to belittle them. Instead she was there...being herself. The color of her skin was different. If nothing else, it set her apart from the bevy of beauties. She told the women, "I am dark but lovely." She is the first one to point out her difference and did not try to camouflage or apologize for it. She knew that she was lovely. Talk about healthy self-esteem! Can you say that about yourself? Note she didn't say, "I don't have fair skin, but I am lovely." She declared, "I am dark." There you go. "You may not think that's great, but I think I'm fabulous." Can you say, "My eyes are brown and I am lovely?" Not, "My eyes are not blue, but I am still lovely." There's a big difference between the two. The first says, I accept myself, I am aware of myself and I like myself. The second says I'm ok, but I think I'd be better if…. Why don't you give it a try right now? Think about that one physical aspect of you that you were always a little dissatisfied with. Now, make an objective analysis of that part whether it's size, color, shape…whatever. Now say it…my boobs are small and I am lovely! My nose is wide and I am lovely! My thighs are substantial and I AM LOVELY! Say it until you feel it and you know it. Say it until you can't help but smile because you truly are lovely. Did you smile yet? If not…say it again and mean it. You were made to inspire awe and arouse reverence to Almighty God for his wisdom in creating a being as complex as you. God is pleased when He sees you because your differences remind Him of His own awesome creativity and goodness. You are His workmanship, His creation, His masterpiece.

Don't let your differences be a hindrance to you. Celebrate everything about yourself that may not be what you would consider perfect. Celebrate in thanksgiving to God for creating you the way He did. I remember the day the realization of whom I was hit me. I was at university in the middle of a class about African American women authors. I sat up and looked at the diversity of people my class represented. In that small cross section of my tropical island, no two people in the class had an identical complexion. I looked down at my hand and saw that I too was different. Some were fairer than me and just as many were darker, but my color was mine. I was born with it because God in His awesome wisdom felt that this was what I should be. My classmates must have thought I had emotional issues because huge tears welled up in my eyes as I remembered trying to buy make up two shades lighter or squeezing the sides of my nose to make it thinner. I was just what God designed. He knew I was lovely in my skin, and finally, I knew it too. And darling, I started celebrating. I stopped trying to look like the people in the magazines and started concentrating on what looked good on me like colors that complimented my beautiful brown skin and dark brown hair. It was as if years of crust had been scraped off of me, and everyone noticed. My professors noticed, my family, friends and really cute guys noticed too! When I learned to accept myself totally and communicate to my God that I thought He did an incredible job on me, it changed my entire attitude. Suddenly, I didn't go into any contest as an underdog, underprivileged or underestimated female. I was an equal, impressive and viable woman of God ready to face challenges and become victorious.

Don't misunderstand me…there were days when I didn't wake up feeling like the queen of Sheba – when my hair had a mind of its own and my bloated belly seemed to need its own taxi fare – but never again did it become a burden to me. I knew what I looked like and I knew I was lovely. God said so and I believed Him. Is there a job you've had your eye on? Don't go to that interview prepared to be prejudged because of your physical appearance. You are a child of the Most High God. There is no man on this earth who can withhold from you what God means to give to you. Thank God for what you look like and dress to compliment your lovely complexion, your distinctive features and everything that makes you unique. Don't try to copy anyone. If you know that you are capable and qualified for that position…don't allow your physical insecurity to rob you of that. If you're worried about the way you look, then it certainly comes across to your interviewer as a lack of self-confidence.

I've often heard people remark, "Wow, she is fine…or she is hot," only to realize that the object of their attention was (by media standards) a not-so-great-looking person. Yet, the confidence that they exude is one of the aspects of their personality that makes them irresistible. It made the Shulamite irresistible to Solomon as well as to the daughters of Jerusalem. That's why in Songs of Solomon 1:5 she compared herself to the curtains of Solomon, dark but intriguing, simple but opulent, soft yet resilient. Solomon's curtains veiled the true majesty of his courts and were closed to uninvited guests. The Shulamite was saying that she too was far more than what they could see with their eyes. She was a woman of substance and conviction. She was intense and profound.

Are you worth someone's time and effort to get to know you? How much is there beneath your surface that's not an attempt to copy someone else? How colorful are you inside and how much of it are you familiar with or even aware of? Are you more than just a pretty face, or is your substance contained in your white smile, immaculate make up and your fabulous outfit? Too many times we think that if we look good then that makes us feel good and that's what people see. Unfortunately, many of us fail to realize, since your make up can fade off, your skin can wrinkle and your great clothes removed, the self-confidence that comes from just looking good in them is superficial. It's temporary and dictates your attitude to an extent that can spoil your entire day and mood if you are bloated or have a bad-hair day. It is great to look good, but it takes more than that to maintain a healthy attitude about the person you are. There is little doubt that the Shulamite was an attractive woman, but she knew that it wasn't a pretty face that would make her the king's chosen. She told the women of the court, "Do not stare at me because I have been darkened by the sun. I may be dark like Solomon's curtains, but that is but a hint of the treasure that is me." Your irresistibility quotient is increased by the value of what's beneath the surface. These are the things that don't change on a daily basis because they're you. It's your internal make up. Your strengths as well as your weaknesses, your virtues and vices, your actual tastes. Actual tastes refer to the things you are truly fond of, not the things you pretend to like because your friends do, or your kids think are cool, or your mate thinks are hot. What are you passionate about? There are things that will stir your soul, make you cry, excite you or encourage you to do something new. Those are the things that make you a colorful woman. You have many layers, a complex mélange of hues and textures that make you an individual. Do you know what they are? Maybe you've been so busy trying to become what everyone wants you to be that you didn't get the time to find out who you are.

Sometimes we don't want to explore who we are because it means dealing with hidden secrets that we repress and try to ensure that no one else finds out. Even the bad things that you've been through are now part of your character. They've changed you and maybe even left scars that seem too deep to fade. But those were circumstances only; yes they left you changed, but there's still enough of you that's stronger than that circumstance. People in your life may have convinced you that you're worth nothing and unattractive. Your life may have been one of hard work, three jobs as a single mom left you no time for yourself, but those are the qualities that God magnifies in you and make you irresistible. Remember when the Shulamite explained, "My brothers were angry with me and made me take care of the vineyards and my own vineyard I have neglected." Scholars suggest that her "vineyard" which she mentioned was actually her own physical appearance and not an actual piece of land. She was too busy working for the benefit of others, and she had no time to look after herself like all the other women had the opportunity to. Sound familiar? Then you are the perfect candidate to be an irresistible woman. You're one that God desires to put in a place of renown and honor, the one He wants people to stare at in awe…wondering and unable to put their finger on exactly what it is about you that makes you so enchanting. Despite the Shulamite's non-conformity to the look of the lovely woman, and the drudgery she had endured, she was the one that the king desired! He called her "the fairest among women" and "a lily among thorns!" Not only did she impress him but also everyone in the court, even the beautiful women called her "fairest among women" in SOS 6:1.

God declares that you are his workmanship, taken from the Greek word *poieema*, meaning His masterpiece. You are God's crowning creation and the apple of His eye and there is no good gift that He would withhold from you. Ask yourself the question: What am I passionate about? I know many if not all of you will say your family or children. What else though? Are you addicted to home improvement and do-it-yourself TV shows? Then apparently your passion is your home, or maybe decorating or refurbishing. Does what's going on with the government incite you or do you tell anyone who will listen your opinion about the war or the crime rate or the level of taxes? Maybe politics is your passion. Do you weep at a live drama, a great song or beautifully choreographed dance? Does a cool spring breeze make you want to throw open the windows and start baking pies? Therein lies your passion. Those are just simple examples of how you can determine what you're zealous about. It's all right to be fanatical about something because that can become an avenue to channel your creativity. Ultimately, your passions make up in large part the person that the world perceives you as.

If you are thinking that you take no great delight in anything and you're just an ordinary "bore"…think again. The Bible explains that whatsoever you need is already in you. You are complete in Him…meaning that being full of Christ you are replete, furnished, imbued and there is nothing lacking within you that God has not provided to be the person that He has chosen you to be. You may not have had the time, finances or energy to pursue your passion, but that does not make its existence moot. It's already in you and God will make opportunities for you to demonstrate it if you would just recognize and ask. God is a miracle-working God, a transforming God. He will take whatever has been a part of you that He put in you for His glory and expand it to glorious proportions if you will let Him.

The desire to preach and teach God's word has been my greatest obsession for many years. I was born the first of three children to my parents in 1975. They were both very young, barely out of school and very poor. My father worked as much as he could, but it was barely enough to feed and clothe them and me. I know there were many nights that my mom went hungry so that I could eat. My parents were also new Christians. They had both been born into Hindu families and brought up in the teachings of that religion. My father was aspiring to become a Hindu pundit and was employed as a Hindu idol maker previous to his miraculous encounter with the Lord Jesus. My mother grew up in a well-to-do Hindu family and was content to remain such until she too experienced the power of Jehovah God. Their love for me was surpassed only by the love they had for their newly found Savior and their hunger to know more of Him. They walked almost two miles to church every time the doors were opened, in rain or sun. They still recall the days when my dad covered his wife, his baby and himself with a huge plastic bag that covered a neighbor's refrigerator and trudged to church in torrents of rain. That was their obsession: to be in God's house...to hear the word of God. The little church was pastored by a little lady, Rev. Samdai, who herself had discovered the awesome love of our Lord Jesus.

Rev. Samdai, at the age of 17 had left her Hindu home at gunpoint for choosing to serve Jesus. She gave up the comforts of her parents and her siblings, a roof over her head and shoes on her feet for the sake of her Lord. She left her home with no destination. All she owned was her Bible and a paper bag of clothes. Through the grace of Almighty God and the obedience of His servants, some of whom had come from the United States, she was able to attend Bible school and graduated class valedictorian even though she had only a 5th grade education. Here, 20 years later, she was the preacher at a packed church that was training new ministers and sending out disciples. She never married and at that time she lived in two small rooms that were contained in the shabby, wooden church building. The church was four walls and a roof; one small 8 x 9 foot bedroom flanked the right side of the "pulpit" area and a similar room on the left served as her office/living room/storage/ dining room/Sunday school class. Her kitchen was a simple, outdoor area behind the church as was her outdoor bathroom. As a newborn, my parents would put me to sleep on her bed in the church, while the service was going on. As the months went by, I grew to love that bed – so much so that I cold hardly fall asleep to anything but the sound of the service and only on that bed. My parents became very involved in ministry at that church and my father had followed the call of God on His life and graduated from Bible school himself. With his pastor's blessing, he was sent to start a church in one of the remotest, poorest, Hindu concentrated and anti-Christian areas of the island. Many men had tried to establish Christian churches there and failed, succumbing to the pressure and persecution that they endured at the hands of the villagers.

My parents would leave me at Pastor Samdai's when they ventured to their new church so I wouldn't have to witness the constant cursing, stoning, death threats, and swarms of mosquitoes that that area was popular for as well as the other diverse tribulations that my parents endured. And, darling, they did endure. That church is still there today, with my dad as the Pastor, as a testimony to the power of God's calling, and it is one of the largest and most powerful churches on the island. While my parents were doing door-to-door witnessing during the daylight hours, walking through marshes and in most uninviting circumstances, Rev. Samdai (my godmother) walked me back and forth to kindergarten. I stayed in the church with her. My playground was the pews and my favorite games were "preacher" and "miracles in service." At 3 years of age, I'd lead the songs, testify, pick up the offering, sing a special song, preach, give an altar call, "fall out" and even get "healed" all by myself. Some nights in my toddler years, I would refuse to leave my godmother even when she preached in the service, and she would continue preaching with me standing next to her holding onto her skirt. I pointed when she pointed, ran when she ran, walked when she walked and shouted, "Amen," every time she did. I had a passion for the things of God that spilled over into my teen and young adult years. My godmother loved me more than any human being; even until the day she died in 2000, she called me "her only child."

Eventually, when my dad's church became more settled, my parents started taking me along. When I was 13, I appointed myself the church choir and youth group leader. These were really unheard of concepts since all the members were converted from Hinduism or Islam and were new to "church." My godmother and my parents had taken me to the U.S. in previous years to the General Assembly of the Church of God where I soaked up every idea about youth and music I could absorb. Then I came home and tried to implement them as well as my childish brain could. Praise be to God, my father let me. He let me be a Sunday school teacher and he encouraged me that whatever my hands found to do for God, do with all my might. I remained a Sunday school teacher, choir director and the youth pastor there until the age of 21. By then the church was several hundred strong, and the choir had won talent competitions and was well known in the Church of God in our country. At 21 I married my wonderful husband Curtis and we moved to Houston where I became the volunteer youth pastor at Woodforest Worship Center. It was a smaller church that could not, at that time, afford to hire a full-time staff member, but my aim remained to do whatever my hands found to do with all my might. God made provision for me to practice my passion. Today I am the full-time, paid youth pastor at that church and I am still in awe of God's wonderful plan.

It doesn't matter where you began or what you've been through. When God created you, you already contained all that would make you an irresistible woman. The key is in recognizing what your passion is and devoting it to the honor and glory of God. Right now, where you are, you can do that. Just tell God, *"Lord, you put in me the love of decorating (substitute appropriately) and now I dedicate that/them to you. Use me and my passion to demonstrate your power and bring glory to you."* One young

Englishwoman once wrote this prayer, "O God, thou puttest into my heart this great desire to devote myself to the sick and sorrowful." She asked him to "give me my work to do." God gave her work to do. This irresistible woman, Florence Nightingale, changed the entire face of medicine and nursing forever… because she recognized her God-given passion and dedicated it to God. As God begins to open doors for you, step through them, search for ways to motivate yourself, enhance what you already know about the subject and always seek to be the best at it. Watch God begin to change you as you become focused and dedicated. Watch people become drawn to you and become inquisitive about you. Be proud of your uniqueness and expect great things when you offer your passion to Almighty God. Celebrate everything that's different about you and watch yourself begin to become irresistible.

"Gimme some bloomin' love" (SOS 2:13)

Marcie had been complaining to her best friend for the last 45 minutes on the phone about how her husband was ignoring her. "I could march around the house in the most tempting outfit and he looks straight past me. I mean, it's as if I'm not even there! Oh, he'll never change." Sound familiar? Sure enough when Jake comes home at 6:30 he and Marcie have dinner, put the kids to bed and then he notices that she is slamming doors and almost stomping about the house. Sure, she's wearing a cute outfit there, but she couldn't possibly be thinking what he thinks she's thinking because that look on her face says that he needs to keep far away. "Oh she'll just blow a fuse if I even try to touch her so I'll just sit here and see what happens; wait till she cools down in a second."

"That jerk, he wouldn't notice me if I had red sirens stuck to my head. He's so insensitive. I'm just not attractive anymore. He probably thinks my legs look like hams, and he's probably wishing he could be with that girl from that TV show…what's her name…." So they both go to bed, she facing the wall and falling off the edge because she doesn't want to touch him. He saying nothing because he knows if he says a word she'll overreact, go berserk, and then start crying and they'll be up until 3 in the morning and he'll be miserable at work tomorrow. And so goes the vicious cycle that goes on until one concedes and then it repeats itself every 3 to 6 weeks.

This common scenario is one of the examples why many people think there is no hope of their relationships and, indeed, their lives getting any better. It seems like every effort you make is a waste of time and energy. Then as one person thinks, "Ok, I'm going to try to do something nice tonight or be sweet and kind…" something goes wrong and someone gets upset and it all goes downhill from there. A feeling of hopelessness sets in. Many women steer straight past irresistibility because we're too busy speeding towards hopelessness. We don't expect our marriage to change, or we do not expect improvement in our job, our school, our relationships, our kids, or our finances. We ignore our husband's feeble effort at romance and make him embarrassed and unwilling to try again. We can take no joy in our accomplishments because they're too small and insignificant to us. Our puny 25-cent-an-hour raise is just trash to us and who cares that I went from a C minus to a B; it's still not an A. This is a serious syndrome of "no bloomin' love."

Bloomin' love is one of the things that God loves most about His church and one of the things that made the Shulamite irresistible to the king. It is love that is offered before you receive what you're asking for. It's loving just because you believe in a promise and not necessarily because you see it fulfilled. It's a love that says, "I have total faith in you that you will do exactly what you said you will do." It's faith that is the substance of things hoped for and the evidence of things not seen. (Heb 11:1) In the Songs of Solomon the Shulamite goes to the vineyard where the grapes have not yet matured. They are not suitable for eating, but the blooms are there. It is at this point, when the blooms are coming out, that the Shulamite offers up her love to her king. Before now, she talked about him and declared her love, but it is at the time of the bloom (when the fruit is not yet mature) that she says, "There I will give you my love." Why are you waiting for the fulfillment of your promise to give God the glory? Why do you say in your heart that, "The day God blesses me with children, or the day I get X amount of money, or the day the doctor tells me this disease is gone from my body is the day that I will fall on my face and worship God...and love Him." Why do we do that? We do it because that is the human nature in us. To give thanks only when we receive what we wanted. The God nature is to say thank you before it's ever in our hands. The attitude of the beloved Shulamite was to offer her love at the first sign of fruit! Lord, I don't have it yet, but, Glory to God, I can almost taste it! God, I haven't seen it yet, but I have your promise.... I see the buds, Lord! I see it! That is what God wants from His beloved. Lord, I don't yet have my complete miracle in my hands but I see the signs, Lord!

In Heb 11:13 Abraham had a promise from God...an incredible promise that he would be the father of many nations. The problem was he was already 90 years old, and to ordinary human beings, that's too old to be participating in conception. Even more improbable was that his wife, 80 years old at that time, would conceive. But the victory was in that, "he believed HIM who had made the promise," so it was, "imputed unto Abraham for righteousness, and he was called the friend of God." What an honor. Abraham's bloomin' love didn't need to see the fruit...just the word was a bloom...a promise. And Abraham in his faith became irresistible to God. Abraham worshiped and loved God when there was no sign of fertility in him or his aged wife Sarah. It was faith's evidence in action. God still looks for those who offer up their love when there is not yet fruit.

As immigrants to the United States, my husband and I have had to face quite a lot of challenges over the past seven years. When we first came here, I worked as the marketing director for a small firm, at least that was my title. Discontent set in after I started working when I saw how much younger people with less qualification and ambition than myself earned more than twice or three or four times what I did. I believed that since I had a bachelor's degree and could speak several languages, I at least deserved a better salary. Since I was the one with the degree, U.S. law only provided for me to work and my husband, who had until then been the major breadwinner in our household, was unemployed. My husband Curtis's dad had passed away when he was 9 and his mother when he was 15 and as the "man" of the house he took up the responsibility to provide a home and a proper education for his three sisters; he worked every day since he was 18 years old. When I met him, he already owned a fully paid for, large house and had a well-paying job. He had security and he liked it that way. Yet now, here we were, following the leading of the Holy Spirit, away from our island home, at a small church in Houston where we were voluntary youth pastors.

My small salary made it very difficult to pay for a place to live, a vehicle, food and utilities but the kindness of our pastors and brethren was always a true demonstration of the love of God in our lives. They always made sure we were taken care of. I was miserable at my job, and my heart never felt at peace because my mind was constantly on ministry and the church. More and more my husband slipped away from me because in my self consumption. I didn't realize that he was going through the most difficult time in his life. Not being able to work not only messed with his ironclad work ethic but also made him question his effectiveness as a true man of God because he couldn't financially support his family – me. The day I took my eyes off what seemed like a hopeless situation and put them back on the promise that God made me...things began to change.

Early on in my time at that particular job, I put my grievances on paper, in as poetic and creative way as I could. It was for my eyes only, in an effort to express some feelings in writing and collect my thoughts ...something I still do, by the way. I described how I felt like a fish caught in a huge net that I couldn't get out of. It seemed I could never be grateful enough. I didn't want to recognize anyone but God as my true source, but I kept finding myself in a place where I felt compelled to do just that. I found almost every reason to be most miserable, and I wrote them down. Well, someone on the job found the short story I had written about the fish in the net and gave it to my employer. When my husband came to get me that afternoon, he was confronted by that employee, and, with his earnest love for me for which I love him so, he vociferously defended my honor. Well, that evening I was fired.

As we drove home in the car, there was complete silence for about 10 minutes and then simultaneously we both erupted into laughter. The car almost shook as we both laughed until tears streamed down our faces. As clear as day, God brought it to our remembrance that we were once again in a familiar place…a place where we were totally dependent on God. The same place we had been 5 years before on our island when God said we should leave and travel to a city we'd never seen. The Holy Spirit visited us in that car and an indescribable peace settled upon us…a peace that had been stolen from me for many years; a peace that wiped away the multitude of tears that I had cried on numerous mornings on my way to work. "We're going home, baby," I said to my husband in more of a question than a statement.

"I don't know," he answered. "I don't feel like God has finished what he has planned for us here." I agreed that I felt the same way but legally, there was no way we could stay in this country, and financially, with no income at all, it was impossible. Ideally, another employer would have had to hire me on the spot for there to be a glimmer of hope, and even so, we would have had several months without income and since we lived paycheck to paycheck that was a negative. Furthermore, as soon as I was fired my ex-employer called the U.S. Immigration offices and informed them that I was no longer under his employ, so I was left no preparation time before I would be required to leave. That evening I received an e-mail from him stating that he called the necessary authorities and found out that I had to be out of the U.S. in two weeks. By that evening however, Curtis and I had already put the situation into the hands of our big God, so there was no fear in our hearts. The only pain I felt was facing my youth group and telling them that we were going home. They had been left by several youth pastors before and some were finally trusting and opening up to God's work in their lives. I hated to make them feel like I had deserted them. The only other persons who knew about this occurrence were my friend, Kim, and my brother, Jason. They prayed and my friend kept saying "God doesn't want you to leave. I feel like something's going to happen today."

That evening the college and career ministers from our little Houston church called to ask us if we would join them for dinner with some friends of theirs who were visiting from out of town. After dinner as we sat around talking, the subject of my work came up and I mentioned that I had lost my job that day. The College and Career ministers were both insistent that they knew God was not finished with us. I felt the slightest bit uncomfortable talking about getting fired, but there was still a peace and lightness about me so it did not bother me enough to not talk about it. The visitor asked me if I didn't mind telling him what I earned and what I considered a "livable" amount of money. I didn't, so I told him and that was that. Well, late that night Curtis and I were praying and declaring the promises to God that He had made to us. My husband was telling God that it didn't matter to him what the situation looked like, for we walk by faith and not by sight. We agreed together that all God's promises were true and yes and amen in our lives, and we believed in a powerful God. We felt abundant joy in the remembrance of God's faithfulness. We were having ourselves a good time thanking God because we could feel in our spirit that He was about to come through. We could smell the blooms of promise and see the buds shooting out and our hearts were filled with glory and praise. In the middle of that, the phone rang and it was my pastor. He called to tell me that someone had delivered him a check for a substantial amount of money with the note that that money was to pay my salary as the full-time youth pastor of that church for a full year! After I was finished jumping up and down on the bed for joy, I told my husband what had happened and we lay there wide eyed for many hours, overwhelmed by the power of God and His awesome love for us. He did not even allow me to go to sleep with the worry of tomorrow. Before the day was done, he answered our prayer with a miracle!

Your victory may seem to be a ways off, but it's still so close that if you try, you can smell it! God's plan for your life is in its early stages…you're on your way. On your way to being blessed, on your way to being healed, on your way to being appreciated, on your way to being recognized, on your way to being the woman that God had ordained you to be…but you can smell the ripening fruit of your destiny. Your business is struggling in green stages but you see the fullness of time. Others may not see it…but you see those buds appearing; you see those blooms force their way out of their seeds to meet the morning air. The love that God has for you is blooming in your life…the grapes are still tender; they are not yet full with the fruit of God's blessing for you; it's in that stage where it may not be good to taste…yet. You can see it, but you can't enjoy it. But hold on! Watch it grow…enjoy the smell. Remember, God is shooting blooms into your crisis, creating blooms that will become fruit, streams that will become rivers, trees that will become forests, stalks that will become harvests, pennies that will become thousands. Bloomin' love is a promise for tomorrow. They are the physical manifestation and testimony of what your eyes may not see, but you know it well. You can smell it!

It is this eager anticipation of fulfillment that thrills the heart of God. It's a magnification of the joy a parent feels watching their kids dance around the Christmas tree, eyeing the pretty presents or shaking them and taxing their brains to see what's inside. This is irresistible to God. It's for the same reason that my husband always gives me a pre-Christmas present. He says he loves the excitement in my eyes when I open presents, especially ones I don't expect. It's what made the Shulamite so irresistible. The grapes were not fully formed yet, but the promise of the harvest filled her with love for her husband, the king. This is what makes you irresistible to our heavenly Father. Your eager anticipation of a promise He made that you believe with all your heart and your desire to praise Him, thank Him, and love Him before it ever comes to pass. It's this attitude of gratitude that touches the heart of God. Saying thank you before your situation changes because you believe that God's word is true. He said that we'd be the head and not the tail and we believe it! He said that he would give us the nations for our inheritance and we believe it! He said by His stripes we are healed, that the wealth of the wicked is stored up for the righteous and our children and grandchildren will be blessed and we believe it! We offer up our love today! Today when these things have not fully occurred yet, when the signs are minute and discouraging to the human eye, we give thanks and praise to the one, true God who is faithful. Like the Shulamite we offer our love and total dedication. This is irresistible to God. It is so much easier and fulfilling to give a gift to someone who is truly appreciative than to someone who couldn't care less. True irresistibility resides in an attitude of gratitude.

So stop griping about your situation. It's more than optimism; it is a firm decision to believe in your dream and to realize that everything you need to succeed is already in you. Do not be daunted by bad news or unexpected circumstances. Thank God for what you are going to do with what He has given you. Thank your husband for being kind and caring, even though all you see now are just hints of that. Thank your kids for being obedient and your parents for their sacrifices. A heart of gratitude is one of the most important traits of the irresistible woman.

I will rise now and seek the one I love (SOS 3: 2)

Search for Him. ARISE NOW! And search for Him. Say, "I will arise now!" Don't remain in your gloom and despair! Refuse to lie passively and accept the trampling of the enemy. Arise now and find your salvation. Find him whom your soul loveth.

Sometimes because of what society, your family, or friends expect of you, you miss the voice of God. The hearing part we have down. We can hear him calling well, but we are limited by what we think other people expect. Your parents told you that you would never amount to anything, society told you that you couldn't amount to anything because you are a single mother, or you live on the wrong side of town, your husband says you're worth nothing, you may think you can't amount to much because of your past or where you grew up, your boss says you're easily replaceable and lucky to have a job....but YOU hear the voice of God. At night as you lay on your bed, you hear the voice of him whom your soul loveth calling you, standing at the door and knocking. The Shulamite said SOS 5:2, "I sleep, but my heart is awake; It is the voice of my beloved! He knocks...." She hears him knocking. You may be in waiting, asleep, still and not moving but your heart is wide-awake. Longing for relief from your situation, from the stress, turmoil and heartache that you're going through so that in the morning you feel like you have not even slept. Even while you sleep you can sense the urgency of the time. You can feel that something great is on the verge of coming to pass. Your destiny is about to be birthed, that weeping may endure, but only for a night because joy will come in the morning. You know because you have already seen the blooms, you have smelled the scent of the sweet rose of Sharon and the lily of the valley. He is near and you can feel Him. Jesus said, "Behold! I stand at the door and knock. If anyone hears my voice and OPENS the door, I will come in to him and dine with him and he with me!" (Rev 3:20)

The Shulamite heard her beloved's voice at the door, but how could she open the door to Him? The rules of society dictated that once her feet had been washed and she was in bed that she couldn't get up and walk around and soil her feet. So she lay there and procrastinated. Some of you have heard the voice of God. He had given you instruction, a Kingdom idea for business or ministry that seemed far-fetched, a way out of your situation that, surely you thought, couldn't be a way out for you! So you procrastinate…you ponder, you get third, fourth and fifth opinions from people who did not listen for God's voice on your behalf and the opportunity for God to reveal the extent of his affection to you passes you by. Have you ever had a thought, that at the moment you had it made you quiver with anticipation? What a great idea! You say to yourself… "I can't wait to tell Ms so and so. Oh, she's going to be shouting the victory with me!" That's what you think, but then you tell her, and she is more than ready to show you all the reasons why it will not work! What a let down. But it was NOT her vision! Not her idea! Not her thought! It was yours. It was God's demonstration of love for you. His knock for you! So you let go of your idea only to see two months later someone else come up with the same idea and become very blessed, or happy, or wealthy and reap the benefits that would have been yours? Whose fault was that? YOURS. You lay in bed and didn't answer the knock of your beloved.

The beloved knocked at the Shulamite's door and for sometime she did not respond. After a while, the Shulamite finally got off the bed and went to the door…but he was gone. The opportunity was missed and her love had departed. At this junction she had a choice. She could take the easy way out and go back in the room, sit on her bed and weep mournfully about her departed lover. So many of us are experts at that, sitting and crying over "what could have been" if I had only done this. We spend more time thinking about "what if's" and ignore the new opportunities as they pass by. The Shulamite could have even gone to her mother and wept and elicited as much sympathy as possible. Many times, this is how we deal with it. We tell everyone who would feel sorry for us and sympathize and tell us it's not our fault that we didn't get what should have been ours! For years I wanted to own a line of bath and body products under the label of Kyria (*lady* in Greek). I designed the packages and labels and chose colors and did everything that didn't require much of a sacrifice. I felt like God had given me that idea, and I wanted to see it become a reality, but I sat on it. I procrastinated and waited and sure enough…a few years later there came another line with the exact type of product that I wanted to have. ALSO, the exact packaging colors, same down to the type face with the only difference being the letter "K." Talk about feeling sorry for myself! My fault…I waited too long; I procrastinated and didn't run with the vision. No one stole my idea; it was simply a great idea that I did not act on, but someone else did. And I cried to my husband and told it to my friends and family until they all knew how cheated I felt. I procrastinated and it was my fault and I wanted everyone to understand my pain. The Shulamite could have behaved like I did and sought sympathy for her loss due to her procrastination. It sure is comforting to have someone tell you how much something is not your fault, even when it really is.

OR…she could have gone back to bed and pretended like he never knocked in the first place. Imagine if she got to the door and he was gone, and she became angry and put off. "Oh, he made me get my feet all dirty and get all the way out of bed and come to the door and now he's not here. Now I'm not even sleepy anymore and my feet are cold. Oh, just wait until I get my hands on him. He'll pay for this. Who does he think he is …can' t he wait a second for me? Am I not worth the wait?"

We do it too. "God, can't you change your schedule to facilitate mine? Why did you have to abandon me God? I just had a few things to settle before I committed to you. I was busy getting comfortable. I was worried about what people would say about me if I answered your call, Lord." Or "I'm mad at God because He promised me something and it didn't happen yet. If God wants me, He knows my address. I'm not asking anymore…I'm tired of asking." An attitude of bitterness and resentment wells up in us and robs us of what God has in store for us.

But none of the above was in the Shulamite's character. Self pity, resentment and bitterness were not at home in her. Had she procrastinated? Yes. Did she let it cripple her? NO. She said, "I will arise now and go look for Him!" She got up and said, "I'll coming running after you. I will not let you leave me; I will not miss your call and your blessing in my life!" She risked her all, including her life, to find him. Are you willing to chase after yours? Are you willing to forcefully run after God's promises? (Matthew 11:12) "The Kingdom of heaven suffers violence and the violent take it by force." It is available to those who will not sit idly by and pine over the past. It is for those with a steely resolve to lay hold on the promises of God. At times hanging onto a dream may seen like hanging from a skyscraper by a string of dental floss but hang on. God is faithful. Keep pushing towards your goal and ignore the minor bumps and bruises on the way. The promises of God are there and they are true, but they are there for the taking. Are you willing like the woman with the issue of blood to press through the crowd? To climb a tree to see the Savior, like Zaccheaus? To surrender your valuable treasure and pour your praise on Him like the harlot? Are you willing to ask and keep on asking, to knock and keep knocking? If you are, then He said in Matthew 7:7 to ask and it will be given to you; seek and you will find, knock and it will be opened to you.

That was the character of the Shulamite: brazen persistence to get hers. She was strong and determined. That is why Solomon in the next verse compares her to Jerusalem, the city of God and "awesome as an army with banners." She is majestic in beauty but powerful, mighty, forceful and effective.

So you defy all the odds. Regardless of what society dictates, of what government statistics say that you need to live below the breadline, of that boss who says you're not worth a penny more than minimum wage, of the school that says your kid is not smart enough to attend there, of the chamber that says you can't own your own business – and you get off the bed. You hear the voice of your Beloved calling you and you go after Him …you open the door and run after HIM. This is another characteristic of the irresistible woman. She recognizes her need and goes after the answer. What do you need today? What does your heart grieve for and your soul cry out to God for? Don't try to hide it anymore, but wake up from your immobility. Make that dream more than just a figment of your imagination and make it a part of reality. Even if your first step is a small one, it is gargantuan progress toward getting what belongs to you.

The irresistible woman is unafraid of getting her feet dirty. Stop looking at all the reasons why you can't do something, why the odds are stacked against you, and go for it. Is your marriage falling apart? Have you given up hope of reconciliation or ever having the loving relationship you once had? Don't give up! Get up off your bed of indifference. Yes, you may think you're simply cushioning your emotions for the wreck that is inevitable…but that's not what God said! He said that man cannot separate what He joined together. Stand on this promise, believe God in an offering of bloomin' love and rise up from your complacency and resolve to find God in your marriage, in your children, in your job, in your finances. The irresistible woman is not a coward. Even in humility, her boldness is apparent; it's not in a brazen or harsh attitude but in her determination to reap what God has promised. She will let nothing defeat her in her quest to get to her Beloved.

When you search for God with all our heart and resolve to find him no matter what, you become irresistible to Him. When you call on His name He will not turn His ear away but will listen and give you the desires of your heart. Say like the Shulamite, "I will rise now and seek the one I love." (SOS 3: 2). ARISE NOW! And search for Him. Don't remain in your gloom and despair! Refuse to lie passively and accept the trampling of the enemy. Arise now and find your salvation. Find him whom your soul loves. Do not lie there and die, but get up and go after your blessing.

Wounded by the watchman (SOS 5:7)

I couldn't wait to go home to tell my husband this awesome idea I had. I knew he just had to be as impressed as I was! This idea was phenomenal! I excitedly waited for him to get home and as soon as he was finished eating, I spilled my idea and made him privy to what I believed to be the mother of all plans! I watched his expression carefully as I spoke, initially unperturbed by the lack of enthusiasm on his face and his changeless yet gentle gaze. By now, I thought, he is supposed to be whooping and hollering and telling me what a genius I am... and slowly, my idea lost its impressiveness as it slipped past my teeth and spilled into the air. Finally, as I stared in disbelief, he mumbled, "That's great, honey." Oh, I cannot describe the agony, the anguish, and the fury that rose up in me. I couldn't believe he didn't get it! I felt like I was cut down at the root. My pride was wounded; my ego deflated...my idea never got off the ground. In retrospect it may not have been as big as I perceived, but it probably would have germinated if I had given it time to incubate in me before shooting it out prematurely. Nevertheless, the simple need for it to be lauded by someone else caused that seed to die.

When you go chasing after your destiny, don't always expect others to cheer you along. Stop thinking that if everyone doesn't agree, then it must not be great. If it caused a stir of excitement in you, then it will do the same for someone else somewhere. It's your destiny, your blessing, your love, your knock, your answer; how can others understand a vision if you are not fully understanding it yourself? It's like the analogy used in Revelations 6:13 about a fig tree that casts its untimely figs when shaken of a mighty wind. The Bible uses this analogy to describe the stars falling from the heavens, but it is also a good one to describe what happens when we allow our dreams to fall away. The figs referred to in this scripture are figs that come out in the winter and fall in the spring, while they are still unripe, when a strong wind blows.

Sometimes the strong wind of doubt, uncertainty, fear and anxiety can cause our dreams to be abandoned and spilled out before they ever get the to stage of maturity. Being irresistible doesn't mean you're exempt from opposition. Oh no, it means just the opposite sometimes; you're a target. It means, however, that you have the fortitude to hold on to what you believe in and to keep your feet planted, so even if you're shaken, you will not be moved.

Expect opposition. Expect it from places you don't expect. In the Song of Solomon, the watchmen about the city, set to protect the city from intruders, thieves and law breakers, saw the Shulamite as she ran after her love. *(SOS 6:7) "The watchmen who went about the city found me. They struck me; they wounded me .The keepers of the walls took my veil away from me."* These were people who were appointed to uphold the law, to protect the inhabitants of the city. Yet, they mistook the motives of the Shulamite. They misunderstood her and most probably judged her character wrongfully, because she didn't conform to their standards. In pursuit of your beloved and your destiny, you will certainly be faced with opposition. Don't expect people to always understand, support or encourage your dream. At times, it's painful when those closest to you do not share your enthusiasm. But this certainly is not the time to abandon your goal. Instead do just the opposite. If you can't find support in people, then do as David did, and "encourage yourself in the Lord." Keep your dream alive…study the word and motivate yourself with the lives of Joseph and Moses who overcame insurmountable odds through the power of God and became mighty in the sight of God and men. Read about other people who have gone after their goals and dreams and made them a reality. Realize that many people set out to accomplish their goals on their own, and some have succeeded in their own ability. Just imagine, your ability as compared to the infinite wisdom, wealth and power of the Creator of this universe. There is nothing too hard for Him to do, and when God gives a vision, He also gives provision! It is this time of travail when you forcefully break the bonds of mediocrity and push towards abundance. It is the time when the enemy will set snares because your deliverance is near. Sometimes even those who are there for your protection will be your greatest opposition to you finding what you're looking for. The ones who, if anything, can direct you to the place where He is, are the ones who sometimes will lead you away or offer no help. "That's too much of a risk," they will advise with good intentions. "You're too old for that." Or, " You're too young to attempt that; don't make yourself a laughing stock." Or, "You know you can't sing." Or, "One person won't make a difference." Or, "A bank won't give you the time of day."

When you finally take that leap of faith and go after the vision God has put in your heart, expect opposition but don't give up when it comes. Many times we chase after an idea with a huff and puff of excitement. We are eager and motivated and we want everything to happen right now. We want to run out to the store and buy 10 canvases and gobs of paint and brushes to get our art studio on the way. After all, we think, how will people buy our art when we have no art to show? Or we head out to the nearest mega store to pick up candle wax and scents for our candle company, fabric and fringes for our fashion house, all descriptions of exotic spices and ingredients for our cookbook. Or our dreams may be more erudite? We buy expensive law texts or subscribe to an expensive medical journal to start "getting informed" for our new career. Or if our goals are more "sanctified" we get an expensive Thompson chain Bible and extra-large, extra-expensive commentaries to go with it. Although our intentions are noble, our actions are hasty and uninspired. Sometimes all we end up with is a deflated ego and a drawer full of stuff we'd be hard pressed to get rid of, even on ebay.

An entrepreneurial spirit is a great benefit if you are chasing after a vision. Wisdom in your actions and sensitivity to the leading of the Holy Spirit, however, is the key to making that gift work in your favor. I myself have learned many hard lessons in my life on listening to God and not making rash decisions. Even as a child, I had a great desire to start some type of moneymaking business. I remember being 5 or 6 years old and during our mid-year vacation from school, I had many days to let my imagination run wild. When I was at my grandfather's house, where my family lived for a many years, I would organize any friends or cousins and my 3-year-old brother, Jason, into a team of "employees" whom I could have in my business. One day I compiled my own newspaper. I called it the *Freeport Express* (since Freeport was where I lived and the Express was a major paper on our island) and it had about 10 pages of news. The fact that the average page size was a 3-inch square did not at all affect my belief that people would rush to buy my paper at 50 cents each! I made 3 whole copies, all in my best crayon handwriting, complete with little pictures to accompany articles. There were articles like "The gas truck (propane) my uncle drives is in the front yard," and "The neighbor went to the store across the street this morning," were on the first half. The next half was the TV-guide, which had the only information I thought people needed: "*Sesame Street* at 3 o'clock." Finally, I made a sign on notebook paper which read "NEWSPAPERS 50¢" and put it up on the chainlink fence facing the street. Then I sat down and waited. I tried to make my cousin and brother wait with me, but they ran out of patience. So I waited alone. Nothing. I went in and had lunch and came back out to the "office" and waited some more. Then, just a short while after I resumed my post, our neighbor Ralph was walking by the house. Ralph was a bit strange and the kids were basically afraid of him, but I saw his eye catch my sign. My heart started pounding. As he began to cross the street approaching me, I felt my heart almost pound out of my chest. He was looking right at my sign. My 3 little newspapers were sitting right there on the bench beside me. His hands came up to the fence as he looked straight at me and asked, "You have papers for sale?" My jaw dropped open, and I sat there stunned for what seemed like an eternity. When I finally jerked back to reality, I jumped up, turned around and ran as fast as my feet would take me straight into the kitchen into my mom's arms and away from my from my first potential customer! "Ma!" I wailed, "Ralph is outside looking for newspapers because I put a sign up saying I had newspapers for sale. But I really don't!" I moaned, "All I have is my little news and I think he wants big news." She laughed. She sent me back to tell Ralph what had happened and she collected several old newspapers to give to Ralph. Turns out he just wanted papers to line old shelves.

My heart was in the right place, but my resolve was weak. I hadn't clearly thought out my strategy or customer service for that matter. Even though that seems like just a humorous childhood story to you, it's one that motivates me to this day to plan ahead, consider all the possible circumstances and have a game plan. Do as it says in Habakkuk 2:2, "Write the vision…write it clearly…" Putting your vision down on paper and establishing it will make it clear to you and allow you to see possible advantages or disadvantages that may arise from taking the course you have in mind. You can iron out quirks and work harder on the things that need more attention. If you don't have the finances, space or time to work on your vision yet…. at least make time to write it down. Speak it in the ears of God and ask for His divine guidance and favor. Pray over the words on the page. Doors will begin to open up to usher you into the fullness of God's promise. If you succeed, then the power you attain by human comprehension may make you attractive to some, but it is not this that will make you irresistible. The irresistibility emerges when you use this "power" for the glory of the name of God and the fulfillment of His purpose. A woman who is self-supporting and uses her own money to meet her needs and accessorize herself and enhance her standard of living is pretty impressive but a woman who could afford absolutely anything she wanted yet gets more satisfaction in using it to give 5000 poor third world children toys for Christmas is amazing. The woman who doesn't only weep but turns her tears into care and nurture for the hurting is an irresistible gem "whose price is far above rubies." There's the self-supported woman who can sing, "See this watch? I bought it….the clothes I wear, the house I live in …I bought it…so I don't want no scrub," and she is commendable, but the woman who gives to others without having to have it broadcast, the woman who fears the Lord shall be praised.

It is uncommon in today's world to find people whose aim is to do only God's will and devote their lives to His service. Many "SAY" they will but their devotion comes with conditions. They will devote their lives to Christ's work if they had enough extra income to live comfortably, or if they don't get into med school, or if they don't get married before 25, or if they can do it the way they want to. People like Florence Nightingale, Mother Teresa and Billy Graham are few and far between. In my years of youth ministry I have watched many young people devote their lives to the service of God in a river of humble tears and continue to watch as they grow up and become so involved in their own lives that that desire is now just a silly childhood moment of vulnerability. Spouses, families, jobs, possessions, vacations, sports, entertainment, even food and everything else in life take precedence over their responsibilities and possibilities in the Kingdom of God. I still wait expectantly and watch as people grow, encouraging them to not let go of the desire that God put in their hearts as children to make a real impact in this world. So they can leave more of a legacy than "he was a good person."

There are two young people in my youth group right now who are very eager to dedicate their lives to the service of God. They want to be missionaries. Ashley and Erin are just two of the many that say it, but I think they are two that might really mean it. They want to tell the whole world about the love of Jesus, starting right here. I want them to. I pray that they don't forget and that they don't become discouraged.

I watch as parents sometimes flinch uncomfortably as their kids mention their desires to be missionaries. They understandably may not care for their children to undergo the hardships, handwork and hard persecutions that usually accompany a calling of this magnitude. They may be afraid that their children's lives will not be "fulfilled" if they don't have ordinary families and a white picket fence and a nine to five and Tuesday PTA. This may be perfect for some, and there are people that are called to be just right there, doing their part for the Kingdom, but when God plants a vision in your heart that will rock the gates of hell and change numerous lives in the love of Christ, this is a call to be regarded. These young people may lose their vision because of the circumstances in their lives, because of obstacles or other opportunities or just becoming otherwise involved...OR...they may hold on to it, overcome every obstacle, fight for the right to preach the gospel and go on the share the truth of God with hundreds of thousands of people. They may fade into the oblivion of everyday people in middle-class America or they may shine to the heights of irresistibility in the Kingdom of God, in this life and the one to follow!

Holding onto a dream in times of opposition is difficult. But this is the true test. This is where you determine whether you will fulfill your destiny or slink back into your protective shell like a scared turtle. Did the irresistible Shulamite abandon her love in her adversity? Did she succumb under the beatings of the watchmen? Absolutely not! Instead, she became more forceful than ever. She declared, "I charge you. O daughters of Jerusalem, if you find my beloved, tell him that I am lovesick!" When you face your opposition, when the battering is too much for you to bear, that's the time to stand and make a declaration to God! Do as the irresistible Shulamite and find someone to help you reach Him when you can't seem to find Him. She could have cowered away like a beaten puppy and said, "Well, at least I tried," but she didn't. She became more determined than ever and sent a message to him by whomever would listen. Sometimes that's what you need. When you've done all you can, find people who can help you find Him. Speak to the prayer warriors and the people who reach His throne in prayer and have them let Him know that you're still searching for Him. "He hears the prayer of the righteous." Oh, what an honor! For your name to be called in someone's prayer unto God. Dear Lord, they will say, "Sharon is trying to find you. She has diligently been searching for you. She is being battered in her search for you, Lord. She is desperate to find you." Oh how it touches the heart of Him that Loves you and already gave His life for you. It grieves Him to see you grieved, for the feeling of our infirmities touches Him and He collects your tears in a bottle. But it honors Him to see your love and desire toward him.

Don't mistake irresistible resolve for infallibility. The irresistible woman is by no means a perfect woman. There comes a time when you need those around you. The Shulamite cried out to the daughters of Jerusalem for assistance. In your effort to be chairman, president, super-mom, housewife of the century or get that promotion or scholarship, you may have developed a steely hard armor that insinuates that you never need anyone's help.

Recognize the time you will need others – others just like yourself who may be in similar situations, or people who you can trust to go before God on your behalf. The Shulamite sent message to her lover with the women who were competing with her for his affection! She was desperate to reach him, desperate to let him know that even though she had not answered the door at his first call, she was here now, searching anxiously to find him. It was no wonder that Solomon couldn't resist her; she risked her own life to find him and reassure him of her love. He was probably receiving messages from all those women of Jerusalem, "Shulamite was looking for you, Solomon. She looked like she was beaten, and she was desperate to find you. She said to tell you that she loves you." How he must have wondered and worried and dreamt about her. There was no way he could have doubted her love for him.

The Shulamite went in search of him, and in doing so she had to strengthen her resolve and brace herself for a fight. You too have to lay hold of your purpose and get ready to fight for your marriage, your children, your future, your sanity, your blessing, your relationships, your nation, your character, your ministry, your witness, your integrity, your good name. It's a common and true saying that "if you don't stand for something you will fall for anything." But don't stand for just anything. Stand up in strength for a passion that God has planted in you. Because, darling, heaven and earth will eventually pass away, but not one word that God has spoken will pass away. Don't be afraid of your fight, my friend. That's the sign of your imminent victory. There would be no opposition from your enemy if you were not a threat. Make your back strong and brace yourself for the night because in the morning there's victory. In Genesis 28 Jacob wrestled all night long with the angel. He held on even after his hip came out of the socket. He didn't see this angel as an enemy; he saw him as an opportunity for a blessing! What a revelation. Look at your adversity as an opportunity for God to bless you. It's almost like those old children's video games where you could finish the level without dying and get 1000 points, but if you killed a monster or racked up some coins, or toppled some turtles along the way, great is your reward at the end of the level: thousands of points and weapons for the next level of the journey.

After the Shulamite is battered and cries out a message to her beloved, she still does not sit and pine and surrender. She has an indomitable spirit of a warrior that will not relent. With all her might, she declares his praise and recites a most detailed description of the beauty of her beloved. She is saying he is worth this trial, You may not understand what he has given me. You probably can't see what I see, but he is altogether lovely! He is my friend, my beloved, and just one glimpse of him in glory will the toils of life repay. The Shulamite's Song is one of praise to her love. Even in her darkest moment, his beauty far surpasses the pain she endures. The hope of his glory is a greater and more excellent reward than anything the world can offer. We can sit and lick our wounds, or we can say like Paul that we count it a joy when we suffer for Christ's sake, knowing that it is not in vain.

The spirit of a woman has been the subject of countless movies, the theme of numerous verses of prose, the topic of many mournful and touching songs. Celebration of women's strength has been the driving force of feminism and most women's movements since recorded history. Yet, despite all the facts we know about the strength, courage, perseverance and will power of women, we still make up the majority percentage of the world's depressed. It seems that our strength gives us the courage to drudge on, but it doesn't give us the hope that our lives will improve. It gives us the strength to fight for our children, but it consumes our will to fight for ourselves. Depression is a thief that robs you of the ability to find hope in small changes and the belief in the truth that GOD is faithful. That may be the way it seems to you, but the TRUTH of the matter remains that God is indeed faithful. Even when we're not...He is. Going after your dreams is a good thing, but there is no greater thing than going after God. When He is the object of your affection, your battle has already been won. Your knocking will lead to an opening. Your seeking will lead to a finding. Absolutely. No exceptions. He replaces your brokenness with wholeness, your mourning with praise and your depression with joy. He said in Jeremiah 29: 13 and 14, "I will be found of you when you search for me with all your heart." And in your earnest searching, you become irresistible to the Holy and Almighty God. You become the object of His affection, His beloved, and His irresistible bride.

Held Him and would not let Him go (SOS 3:4)

After what she had been through, it was impossible for her beloved to remain unchanged. He had thought that she was perfect and beautiful before this point. He had praised her physical beauty, her spotlessness, her physical attributes that were natural; she really had little choice but to be beautiful. After her ordeal, however, his compliments changed into a more glorious praise. No longer was she simply the most beautiful among women, but there was a more lasting and impressive and thrilling allure to her. She was beautiful, but she was strong: A tower of determination, strength and resilience that made her beloved delight.

Praise of an irresistible woman may begin in the beauty of a face or the sweetness of a smile, but it never stops there. The irresistible woman is a complete package. Many of us focus so much on what people can see that we neglect the more important things. Probably one of my least favorite things is the look of a disgusted or angry woman. I know you all can see it now. That snarl and glare that she casts in the direction of the object of her disgust. Even worse are those times when we do that and think the other twelve people in our company can't tell that we are displeased and that our target is the only one affected. How discomfiting it is to be in the presence of a woman who just gave her husband the "we'll talk about this later" stare-of-dread and then turns right back around and smiles at you. How irresistible can that be? All the men think, "I'm glad I'm not going home with her." Some women think, "Poor guy." Others may think, "Oh, he deserves it," and the guy: he is either embarrassed and smiles it off, silent to avoid a bigger scene, or maybe he is even angry. Either way, the last thing on anyone's mind is beauty.

I'm almost disappointed sometimes when I look the young ladies I teach or mentor and see them almost attain to a level of incredible beauty, maybe even irresistibility, and then allow something to snatch that away. One young lady I know is an almost perfect package. By any standard, she is incredibly beautiful: perfect hair, teeth, skin, eyes, body...you name it, she has it. Not only that but she is very talented and exceptionally intelligent. She's kind, considerate, funny and patient. Irresistible...almost. She started keeping the company of people who were less considerate towards others. Now even though her face, body or personality has not changed, you can hear and see the difference in her. Subtle jokes about someone else's clothes or odor were never a part of her character. Petty bickering with friends about another young woman, though seemingly harmless, has robbed her of potential irresistibility. Even though she may have made a closer friend in a gossip partner, she may have forfeited a far greater prize...the one attained by the Shulamite...the object of her greatest desire.

In an attempt to please others, many of us lose ourselves. We please friends, parents, relatives, employers and leaders all day long. My father always advised me to "trust God and love people" because people are only human. Irresistibility is not infallibility. Humans fail. God never does. Many of us fall short of our targets because we try to force ourselves into perfection. That's like trying to fit a size ten foot into a size six glass shoe. All you end up with is a painful mess. We hold onto a vision of perfection in our head that sometimes depends on a six-figure income or a size-four figure, and we punish ourselves mentally for falling short. We lose sleep thinking of ways to achieve these and lose joy when we don't have bright ideas. When we come to realize who we are in God, our self image, the way He sees us, things will change. This is not about self-esteem. We all know the advice about healthy self-esteem and what it can do...but the Bible actually teaches us to "esteem others more highly than ourselves." It also teaches us, however, to see ourselves as we truly are in God's sight: beloved. We are His crowning creation and the apple of His eye. Forget trying to become and just enjoy being. Stop worrying about tomorrow, and realize that in God's eyes your dreams have all come true because He has already seen your tomorrow. He knows how your story ends. Doesn't it seem reasonable to trust the One who knows and give up the hassle of trying to figure it out on your own?

When you've given up these burdens, then you are free to wrap your arms around your future, your loved ones, and your dreams and hold on tight. When the Shulamite finally found her love, she said, "I held him and would not let him go." This is the spirit of the irresistible woman. After you've worked so hard and waited so long, why would you give up now? As your irresistibility begins to shine through, you may be tempted to stop at "enough." You'll love most people, but you can't stand that girl. You don't exactly know why. Give it up. All it will do is stand in the way of your dream and your irresistibility.

...I FOUND PEACE (SOS 8:10)

In the age of what I call fake feminism, you'd be hard pressed to find a woman who is at peace. I do not necessarily mean a peaceful woman but one who is at peace with herself. Feminism has fooled us into thinking that a strong woman is a militant one. Our woe-is-woman mentality has caused many of us to look cynically at the world and see ourselves as underdogs and almost carnivorous animals that must scrape and fight to get what is ours. I certainly do not intend to undermine or underestimate the achievements of strong women who have paved the way for the freedoms we enjoy in a world that is unfair. But I do intend to denounce the actions of those who continuously strive to cause hatred among people and make some women feel more victimized than they are. In an attempt to "empower" women to become better, they have instead crippled women with a victim mentality and placed an unwarranted fear in the hearts of many. When one woman, Madalyn Murray O'Hair, can have such an influence in removing public prayer from the school system of the democratic United States of America when the majority millions of women who disagree with her sit back and watch hopelessly, she has not liberated women. She made them social cripples. They are just women who are afraid to stand up for what they believe because they feel too insignificant to fight the system. An irresistible woman understands that there may be times when her plans may not work out the way she hopes...but they will work out. Not only will they work out but also they will work together...all the seemingly disjointed pieces of life will work together, for her benefit. I once heard someone ask the question, "If you were absolutely certain that you would succeed at anything you did, what would you do? I'm sure many of us would do things we have never even considered before. Well, this is exactly the promise that we have in Christ! In Psalms chapter 1, the Bible says that WHATSOEVER we do will prosper! An irresistible woman knows this truth. She is not afraid to attempt the task that looks like it's sure to fail because her guarantee is the word of Almighty God.

Instead of spending night upon night worrying about whether you should take that leap of faith, trust that God has a plan for you. Trust that if you fall He is always there to catch you and bear you up on the wings of eagles. This is where peace comes from…knowing that this is a win-win situation. Either way, you can't lose. On the one hand, if it goes the way you want, your dream would have come true. If it doesn't, then God has a bigger and better plan for your future. The Shulamite could have fretted about looking unkempt because she had spent all her time caring for her brother's vineyards. She could have griped and pleaded her case and even gotten her brothers to give her a break! Then for certain she could pamper herself and at least stand a fighting chance competing against the other beauties for the affection of the handsome king. What a dream come true! But she didn't do that and God understood why. The plan was for Solomon to look past just the physical beauty and see the irresistibility that was part of her.

In the Shulamite's quest to getting to her love, she did not trample on or push aside anyone else. This is one aspect of the irresistible woman that can sometimes feel like swimming upstream. How do we attain our goals without pushing anyone else down, even unintentionally? The answer is in your motive and process. If your pursuit is for selfish gain, then you have already defeated yourself in your attempt to be irresistible. Selflessness, humility and an attitude of gratitude are all aspects of the irresistible Shulamite. For some reason some women think they can improve their worth in someone's eyes by putting down another. Even as children we usually come to the understanding that this does not work. If we know it, then why does it continue? It runs in the social arteries of our education system at every level, even regretfully at postgraduate levels. It seeps into the business, recreational and even religious places in our lives. The need to make ourselves look good is often satisfied at the expense of suffering another person's physique, personality, possessions or persuasion. It may be something as trivial as, "Sure her car may be a luxury sedan, but you'd have to be pretty clueless to not buy an SUV with the kind of roads we have here in Texas," or "That is a pretty color, but it makes her look washed out…like a ghost…doesn't it, honey?" to more offending and consequential statements. Very quickly, this evil snatches all hints of irresistibility from you and even if your listener agrees with your statement, you have forfeited your chance to be irresistible in their eyes. Yes, even if they agree. Gossip in any form, fun or hateful or girl talk, is unattractive.

Exciting yes, fun maybe, but it lowers your esteem in the eyes of the listener. It's like a little nagging let down that won't change their love for you, nor their mind, but irresistibility is long lost. Now you're just great... just like everyone else.

The Shulamite never said a single ill word about the daughters of Jerusalem. The only comment she made to her love about them was to tell him that she fully understood why they would love him. To her it was impossible not to love him. "Rightly do they love you," she said. She couldn't blame them for wanting him. An irresistible woman knows when to give praise where praise is due. To her family, friends, classmates, co-workers and even acquaintances. Give praise to those who deserve it even if they're your competition, because you're honest, confident and unafraid. Understand that a compliment to another person IS NOT a criticism of yourself and certainly don't include the latter in your compliment. You know, "WOW, your teeth are so white. I know mine look like old wheat bread," or something to that effect. That is not a compliment! Although you may get a laugh from the listener, you have almost implied that they should feel guilty about having white teeth plus you put yourself down! The most unattractive woman is one who constantly puts herself down. In fact, that trait is unattractive in men as well as women! I chuckle every time I remember my father in front of the mirror. As a girl I remember looking at him comb his hair or trim his moustache and I remember him quoting the words from an old poem, "I am the monarch of all I survey. My rights there are none to dispute." He did it quite convincingly, too. It made me laugh. He still has a pretty healthy self-image.

Being at peace with yourself is understanding who you are in Christ Jesus, understanding that He sees you as a masterpiece. Being at peace with others is in not seeing everyone as your competition, but appreciating the differences in them and remembering that they need affirmation as much as you do. Being at peace with God is in making Jesus, the Prince of Peace, the Lord of your life. The peace that He brings surpasses comprehension because to the eyes of those around you, it shouldn't be so. How could you have peace when you're in the middle of a divorce, or you're failing geometry, or you just lost your job? Only one way, by taking all your stuff, worries, problems and concerns and dumping them on Jesus. Yes, I said dumping them. Not scrutinizing each one and analyzing each one to death but ditching it in one huge heap into the lap of God. "Well, that sounds rather presumptuous and offensive," I can imagine some of you thinking right now, but I'm telling you that's what He asked us to do. "Cast your burdens onto Jesus for He cares for you!" The word "cast" means to throw, fling, toss, pitch, chuck.... you get the idea. This surrender will not only give you peace of mind, but it will help erase those dark circles under your eyes and worry lines on your forehead as well! Need some help doing that? Well, it's as easy as dropping immediately to your knees right now, (it's the first sign of surrender), lift your open hands (the second), and say as loud as you can, "I give up, Lord! (the third) You take it. Here are my finances. Here's my husband, my children, my dead-end job. I'm giving it to you...it's not my worry anymore, Lord. It's yours. You take my burden and I'll take your peace in Jesus's name." Just cast it.

An irresistible woman is at peace with herself. That inner turmoil that causes angry outbursts for no reason, or unwarranted hatred or jealousy, is not a part of her. When you have found peace, it shows. The relaxed jaw, bright eyes, ability to give undivided attention, gentleness, warm smile are all signs of your peace. It goes further than a new dress, great hair or three nights of yoga a week. All of those are transient. When the Shulamite says, "I found peace," she had found herself in her lover's arms, not running, looking or chasing. The grapes were now ripe and ready for harvesting. That which she had been grateful for along time ago was finally here. She was certainly *impossible to resist or withstand the force or effect of, or impossible to refuse, oppose or avoid because too pleasant, attractive and strong.*

Printed in the United Kingdom
by Lightning Source UK Ltd.
104178UKS00001B/80